DAYS THAT CHANGED THE WORLD

ROGER CARSWELL

10 Publishing
a division of 10 of those.com

First published in Great Britain in 2023

British Library Cataloguing in Publication Data
A record for this book is available from the British Library

ISBN: 978-1-914966-94-1

Designed by Pete Barnsley (CreativeHoot.com)

Cover background image: Artem Sapegin on unsplash

Printed in Denmark

10Publishing, a division of 10ofthose.com
Unit C, Tomlinson Road, Leyland, PR25 2DY, England

info@10ofthose.com
www.10ofthose.com

1 3 5 7 10 8 6 4 2

Contents

1

They are unforgettable days

During the First World War the then Prince of Wales was invited to a special hospital on the outskirts of London. Three dozen of the most wounded men from the front were being cared for. He agreed to pay a visit.

On arrival, he was shown over the principal ward. He shook hands with some, spoke kind words to many and sympathised with them all.

'I thought there were thirty-six,' the Prince of Wales said, looking around as his visit drew to an end. 'I have only seen thirty.'

It was explained that six of the very worst cases were in a special side ward not usually visited.

'I must see them,' he said.

Guided by the doctor into the side ward, he saw the men, bruised, maimed, helpless wrecks.

But there were only five.

'Where is the other?'

It was again explained that one poor man was so badly injured that he was kept in a room alone and it would be wiser not to see him.

'I must see him too,' he said.

Taken into the room he saw a sight which stunned him. There lay all that was left of a brave soldier. He was blind, deaf, legless, armless and disfigured almost beyond recognition as a human being. Standing silent a moment, moved beyond measure, the Prince of Wales stooped down to kiss the brow of the veteran, and with trembling voice he exclaimed, 'Broken for me!'

Throughout history, there are many stories of people who have given their lives on behalf of others. Every remembrance of heroism and sacrifice deeply touches us. 'Greater love has no one than this, than to lay down one's life for his friends' are the immortal words of Jesus.

Hope for ever

There are days which are indelibly written on our memories. Those who were alive know exactly where they were when they first heard about 9-11. But with the passage of time, even that will fade into a blur and will be known only by students of history.

And yet, the days we remember at Easter are still known the world over as we recall the greatest sacrifice and drama in all of history. The most significant event in history was not the creation of all things, nor even the moment when the Creator came into our world and was born in Bethlehem. The most significant event of all time can be dated to the first Easter, when Jesus suffered and died, was buried and then rose again from the dead, leaving behind an empty grave and a changed world.

Easter does not have the razzamatazz of Christmas, but it completes what Jesus started when He was born into the world thirty-three years before. We can't have one without the other. In fact, not only did Jesus repeatedly foretell that He would suffer and die on a cross, He said that His death was the fulfilment of all that the prophets that came before Him had spoken about down the centuries.

Easter eggs and bunnies may put a smile on our faces, as well as inches on our waistline, but they betray the huge significance of Easter. Jesus' death was the ultimate sacrifice. His resurrection was the ultimate victory. A way was opened up for men and women to enter into a relationship with God which would last for ever. This is what Easter is all about. Easter is the only hope which doesn't evaporate like a vapour with the passing of time.

2

They were long-anticipated days

In November 1922, Howard Carter cleared debris from the entrance to some tombs in Egypt. He was an archaeologist who for many years had been excavating and exploring in Egypt. As he slowly cleared a staircase, he discovered some intact royal tombs.

'What do you see?' his sponsor asked as Carter broke the seals and looked in.

'Wonderful things,' he replied.

Howard Carter had made the greatest archaeological discovery of that century as he opened up the tomb of Tutankhamun.

One story

The world's bestselling book, the Bible, is full of wonderful things. They are not sealed but available to be discovered. The Bible is packed with history, biography, wisdom and poetry. It contains law and letters, guidance and the Gospels, sermons and songs. It warns of the seriousness of sin but provides the remedy. It speaks of the beginning of time and describes the end of this world as we know it. It reveals who God is, and who we are. It shows us what God has done, and what we should do. It avoids fake news and refuses to airbrush its heroes. It has great comfort but makes uncomfortable reading for those who prefer life without God.

The Bible was written over a period of 1,600 years by about forty different authors from varying backgrounds: kings and peasants, aristocracy and paupers, emerging from an Egyptian culture as well as Roman, Hebrew and Babylonian. Amazingly, there is a single storyline. There are sixty-six books in the Bible; the Old Testament contains the thirty-nine books written before Jesus was born and the New Testament is home to the twenty-seven authored after His birth. There is total unity in all that is written.

You would expect some sort of contradiction of ideas and statements, but it all blends together perfectly. So, although the Bible can be described as a library of books, in truth it is one volume. It is God's written message to humanity. He inspired the minds of the authors so they each gave us His word in their own unique style.

Entering the story

A few years back, I heard comedian Lee Mack being interviewed on BBC Radio's 'Desert Island Discs'. He, like all other guests on that programme, was offered the Bible for his 'desert island'. He commented,

> *I'm glad you get the Bible, because I would read the Bible. I think it's quite odd that people like myself, in their forties, are quite happy to dismiss the Bible, but have never read it. I always think, if an alien came down and you were the only person they met, and they said, 'What's life about? What's earth about? Tell us everything,' and you said, 'Well, there's a book here that purports to tell you everything. Some people believe it to be true; some people [do] not believe it [to be] true.' 'Wow, what's it*

like?' and you go, 'I don't know, I've never read it.' It would be an odd thing wouldn't it? So, at the very least, read it.

When you open the pages of the Bible, you enter *the* story that makes sense of who we are and why we're here. In the opening pages we read about how God made us but how, almost from the very beginning of time, our first ancestors defied God and chose instead to discover evil. Yet at that very moment of rejection, God began making wonderful promises. He promised that He would send One who would come and fight evil. This One, a descendant of our first parents, would 'bruise the head' of the devil, Satan, crushing this enemy of God who seeks to destroy humanity. The death blow, however, would come at great cost to the One sent from God. And so, with this first great promise, the starting pistol had been fired. Over the next centuries God would speak of a coming One who would suffer and die, taking on Himself the sin of the world and making a way back to the relationship with God that humans were created to enjoy.

The oldest book in the Bible is the Book of Job. It deals with the issue of human suffering. Job has lost everything – his wealth, health and family. So-called friends try to comfort him with their arguments, not realising that explanations do not heal a broken heart. These friends only added to the torture by their reproaches. However, in response, Job answered the unkindness by saying, 'For I know that my Redeemer lives, and that He shall stand at last upon the earth.' Centuries before the birth of Jesus, Job was confident of a coming Redeemer and His ultimate victory. As the Bible drama unfolded, the vision of this Person becomes clearer.

Perfect predictions

As you read through the first few books of the Bible, there are many picture portrayals that dramatically depict what would happen when this Redeemer came. There are many parts that can seem very strange to our twenty-first-century minds, but they are important and relevant to us. They foretell the events of Easter and its significance.

The Bible particularly focuses on God's interactions with one people group, the Israelites. They, like us, were conscious of wrongdoing in their lives. In fact, they would have probably had an even clearer view of their sin as God had directly given them His law. Imagine an Israelite, painfully aware they had neither loved the Lord their God with all their heart, soul and mind, nor their neighbour as themselves. And yet they wanted to be right with God, and knew they needed forgiveness. What could they do? They could follow the instructions given by God and take a sacrifice to a Jewish priest. The Israelite would lay their hand upon the head of the animal, often a goat or lamb, before it was killed. By laying a hand on the substitute, a person symbolically transferred their guilt to the sacrifice. It would die in their place. It would carry their sin, and exchange its life for theirs. Sin always brings death – either the death of a substitute or the death of the sinner. Every lamb, every sacrifice, was portraying the fact that in the fullness of time, One would come who would take on Himself the sin of the world.

As the Bible progresses, there are many hints and pictures of a coming King and Redeemer. A Ruler would come from Bethlehem (Micah 5:2). God's Servant would open the eyes of the blind (Isaiah 53:5). A King describes terrible suffering, which includes His hands and feet being pierced while His clothes are gambled for (Psalm 22). One would come who would take the sin of the people and be killed, and yet somehow still triumph (Isaiah 53). The whole of the Old Testament points forward to a Saviour, who would be 'led as a lamb to the slaughter' to do the great work of saving many.

A prophet called Malachi, writing at the very end of the Old Testament, tells the reader of another promise from God. The Lord God will send a messenger ahead to prepare the way for the One who will provide refining and cleansing. And so the people waited. Finally, at the beginning of the New Testament, years later, a man called John the Baptist, began preparing the way. When he saw Jesus, John proclaimed, 'Behold! The Lamb of God who takes away the sin of the world!' The Redeemer had come.

The fulfilment

It is noticeable that those who ridicule Christianity, whether in the media, in books or in lecture theatres, can never explain how what happened in a moment of history had been so accurately pictured and foretold centuries before. The more a person reads the Bible, the more obvious it is that the whole of the Old Testament points to Jesus, laying out all He would be and all He would do.

Jesus claimed to be the fulfilment of all the pictures and the prophecies of the Old Testament. He lived a spotless life. He worked miracles that someone who was an imposter could never do. He spoke to God, and called Him His 'Father'. He said He was God, come in human form to be the Mediator between God and people. He took on Himself the very sacred name of God using the words 'I AM', the precise name that God had given Himself centuries earlier in the Old Testament.

It didn't take long for the religious establishment to get very uncomfortable about all Jesus claimed. Jewish people would, rightly, never use God's name for themselves. When Jesus did, they tried to stone Him to death, not understanding that Jesus was the only One who had a right to do so. It was this, combined with jealousy, fear and insecurity, which led to the religious leaders plotting to have Jesus crucified. They were consumed with the desire to get rid of Him. The die was cast.

3

They were the cruellest days

As a teenager I looked forward to the weekend. About 100 teenagers would get together on a Friday night for a Christian gathering just around the corner from Headingly Cricket Ground in Leeds. I am sure we were more enthusiastic than all the Yorkshire cricket fans. On Saturdays we met together in the home of the leader of the group, Professor Wright, a deeply committed Christian who taught medicine at Leeds University.

One of his favourite stories was of a Russian officer who had got into deep debt and feared that the merciless despotism of the empire would show him no leniency. By candlelight, at his little table in his tent, he was poring over his accounts in despair. He wrote the words, 'Who can pay so great a debt!' and resting his head on his arms fell asleep.

Later, the Czar himself passed by and noticed the sleeping officer. Glancing curiously at the page, he saw the desperate words. Taking up the officer's pen the Czar wrote underneath, 'I, even I, Alexander'. Professor Wright would go on to explain the debt we all owe to God, and of a Ruler greater than the Czar who has paid that debt. He would quote the couplet,

I owed a debt I could not pay;
He paid the debt He did not owe.

The debt

We have been given a life by God our Maker. We know there are many uncertainties in life, but whatever our situations we are not living as we ought. Frank Sinatra may have sung about having too few regrets to mention, but most of us are aware of words we wish we had never spoken, deeds we ought not to have done, things we've got involved with that we should have avoided. When things go wrong, it is easy to ask, 'Where is God?', but when things are going well we choose to distance ourselves from Him and ignore Him. Sin, both our wrongdoing and the way we ignore God, is serious. It cuts us off from God; it would keep us out of heaven, and it would condemn us to hell. Our holy God hates sin, and His justice demands that a penalty has to be paid for wrong. He cannot merely overlook our rebellion. It has devasting consequences and needs to be dealt with.

God has revealed Himself in His word, the Bible, as being absolutely pure and holy, and shown us to be sinful. It is an innate condition that leads us to deliberately go the wrong way. And it is our sin that has severed our relationship with God in the first place. How can a pure, perfect God meet freely with people who have deliberately turned their back on Him?

A difficult diagnosis

I love the honesty of the Bible. Jesus told it as it is. A little while ago I was diagnosed with cancer. The surgeon was honest with me. He told me it would be life changing, then put the options before me. I am not a medic and really wanted his advice as to what should be done next. I certainly didn't want things just to be left to worsen. I took his advice and went through the procedures.

God has never made a mistake on His diagnosis of what is wrong. He lays before us the options, but it would be foolish to leave things when there is a foolproof remedy available. The tragedy is that many decide to 'self-medicate'. All other religions of the world are seeking to help people remedy their own malignant condition. Religions give us lists of what we should try to do and achieve in the hope that they might bring us to their god. Christianity teaches us that we can never get up to Almighty God: He is too holy and too great. Rather, He has come down to us. He came to reach, rescue and redeem us.

The mission

Occasionally a person might come up with an ambitious mission statement for their lives. Three hundred years before Jesus was born, Alexander the Great set out to conquer the whole of the Persian Empire. He desired revenge, fame and glory. Jesus' mission statement was very different:

- *'I have come to seek and to save those who are lost.'*
- *'I have not come to call the righteous, but sinners, to repentance.'*
- *'I came not to be served, but to serve and give My life as a ransom for many.'*
- *'I am the Good Shepherd; the Good Shepherd lays down His life for the sheep.'*

There is no doubt that Jesus lived a life that is above the ability of anyone else to live. He lived such a sinless life that even His enemies could not fault Him. He made the blind see, the deaf hear, the mute speak. He cured the paralysed and cleansed the lepers of their alienating disease. He cast out demons. He instantly calmed a ferocious storm at sea. He fed thousands with just a few loaves and some fish. He raised the dead back to life.

His greatest work was done in a few dreadful hours outside the city walls of Jerusalem at a place called Golgotha, the place named 'the skull'.

Betrayed

Just a few days earlier Jesus had been hailed as King. There had been times when Jesus had deliberately withdrawn Himself to quiet places. There had been occasions when the people would have made Him King, but their plans had been thwarted by Jesus Himself. But eventually it was His time. The Jewish High Priest had passed an edict commanding that information be given as to Jesus' whereabouts. Nevertheless, with unsurpassed courage, Jesus rode publicly into Jerusalem on a borrowed donkey. Because Jesus was to die for the sins of the world, everything had to be done in full view. Publicly, He preached knowing that in a few days He would be publicly brought to trial; and, of course, He would then be publicly taken to the cross and crucified.

After a few hectic days of preaching and activity in Jerusalem, Jesus was betrayed by one of His disciples. Judas loved money and sold Jesus for the price of a slave, just thirty pieces of silver. Jesus was arrested in a place that Judas knew He often went to pray alone. Judas pre-arranged the sign to identify and betray Jesus – a kiss. Deep remorse later overtook Judas, who threw back the silver and hanged himself, casting himself into even deeper darkness. He never witnessed what Jesus was born to do, and what had been planned in eternity before 'the foundation of the world'. Jesus however, had no regrets about being in that olive grove. Reading the Gospel accounts of His arrest, it is apparent that He was in total control of all the events that unfolded, including His own arrest. Even the soldiers fell back when confronted with Jesus and wouldn't have been able to arrest Him if He had not allowed it.

Crucified

What Jesus endured from then onwards is beyond imagination. He had a series of mock trials. They scream out injustice. Where else would you hear a judge say 'I find no fault in Him' but then hand Jesus over with the order to 'Crucify Him'? The religious leaders wanted rid of Jesus whatever the truth and whatever the consequences. Their appearance and status masked the hypocrisy that often accompanies the power hungry.

Jesus was mocked, spat upon, jeered, beaten and lashed. His sensitive brow was crowned with thorns wedged on His head. On His lacerated back He was compelled to carry the rough, rugged, Roman cross to the place of execution. When He was severely weakened, a man from Cyrene was forced to carry the heavy cross the rest of the way, bearing its weight in place of Jesus. I have often wondered why none of the disciples, and not one of those who had been healed, transformed, forgiven or even just fed by Jesus, volunteered to carry the cross. But things were happening so quickly for those bewildered followers and as Jesus staggered past, they were filled with fear and confusion.

The Bible spares us the gory details of what crucifixion meant to the victim. We know His hands and feet were pierced with nails. We know He was lifted up on a cross. We know of just seven short sentences He said as He suffered there. He prayed for forgiveness for His persecutors; He took loving care of His mother; and He promised paradise to the thief crucified next to Him.

'Lord, remember me when You come into Your kingdom,' the tortured thief had begged.

'I say to you, today you will be with Me in Paradise,' Jesus assured him.

On the cross, Jesus spoke of His thirst, and of His forsakenness by His Father, before praying, 'Father, into Your hands I commit My spirit.' His very final statement resonates to all humanity for all time. In His language, He spoke just one word: 'Finished!' We translate it into three words: 'It is finished!'

Accomplished

As Jesus cried out 'It is finished!', His greatest work was accomplished. There is so much meaning contained in those three words:

- *The ultimate sacrifice had been offered.*
- *The work of paying for sin was complete.*
- *The way of reconciliation between God and humanity had been made.*
- *The door to heaven had been opened wide.*

For the three hours before this cry, God had sent a deep, tangible darkness over the face of the earth while He had taken the sin of the world and laid it on His darling Son, Jesus.

With His blood He paid the price to ransom lost humanity. Amazing things happened during the period of deep darkness: there was an earthquake in Jerusalem, graves opened, and the heavy, huge veil in the temple tore from top to bottom opening the way to God. The meaning of all this has been astounding people for generations.

4

They are the most significant days

Dian Fossey was an unusual woman, an American-born zoologist who left the comforts of home to move to Africa. There she lived among the rare, gentle mountain gorillas of Rwanda, who were threatened with extinction due to the cruelty of poachers who were tracking them down one by one and slaughtering them.

In 1967 she established the Karisoke Research Centre in Rwanda, on the side of a 14,000-foot tall, rain-shrouded volcano, and after several years the gorillas came to accept her as one of their own. Fossey named them, cradled their babies and cried with them when they mourned their dead. She once wrote:

> *These powerful but shy and gentle animals accepted and responded to my attentions when I acted like a gorilla. So I learned to scratch and groom and beat my chest. I imitated my subjects' vocalizations, hoots, grunts, and belches, munched the foliage they ate, kept low to the ground and deliberate in movement.*

After spending many years with the gorillas, she became like them, dwelling among them, and they were her friends. When faced with danger, she bravely defended them.

In the early hours of 27 December 1985, she was knifed and murdered apparently by poachers whose trade she had sought to destroy. She died for those she had come to live among and save.

Jesus did more. He came to save, and willingly and deliberately laid down His life for us.

Good Friday?

As He was being crucified, Jesus had prayed, 'Father, forgive them, for they do not know what they do.' As His sufferings came to an end, He prayed, 'Father, into Your hands I commit My spirit.' But whilst He endured the darkness of the cross and bore the heavy load of our sin, He did not address God as 'Father'. Instead He cried out, 'My God, My God, why have You forsaken Me?' In a way beyond our comprehension, as Jesus carried our sin, the intimacy between the Father and the Son was severed. God the Father turned away from God the Son.

'My God, My God, why have You forsaken Me?' are heart-wrenching words. Jesus was forsaken by His Father. He was forsaken by God so that we could be forgiven and never forsaken by Him. People speak of 'Good Friday'; it is good only because, out of extreme love for us, Jesus bore our sin and paid a debt we could not; all eternity would not be sufficient for us to clear it.

About 600 years before Jesus' crucifixion, God told His people that 'I have loved you with an everlasting love.' As Jeremiah the prophet shared these words with the people, one wonders how much he understood about how eventually the eternal Son of God would come to the people He had made in order to bear the penalty for their rebellion against Him.

Sin is so serious it has eternal implications and an eternal penalty. The Bible compares it to a thief, a debt, a heavy burden, a wound, a plague, a deadly poison, a sickness, an abominable vomit, uncleanness, a sting and even to grey hairs! Either we who are finite would suffer the penalty for our sin eternally, or we trust in God's remedy of forgiveness for it. Jesus the eternal One paid the penalty in a finite period of time on the cross. As the divine Son of God clothed in humanity, Jesus was able to carry all the sin of the world on Himself during those hours. If He was only human, that load would have been too great to carry, but as the incarnate God He was able to die to 'reconcile all things' to God the Father.

Justice

If you can, picture the British Airways or Air France plane, Concorde. The front conical nozzle was designed to pierce the atmosphere taking all the friction and heat onto itself to protect the rest of the plane. That nozzle is called 'the propitiator'. The Bible says that Jesus is 'the propitiation for our sins'. A propitiator takes the wrath onto Himself to protect the would-be recipient. God is rightly and justly angry at sin. Jesus, as the substitute sacrifice endured the cross as He took the judgement that should be ours onto Himself. He is the propitiator.

No one has ever faced justice for the murder of Dian Fossey, although all the evidence pointed to the poachers Fossey had relentlessly fought against. One team member, US citizen Wayne McGuire, was convicted *in absentia* but there is widespread consensus that the true culprit was never found. When terrible wrongs go unpunished, we are rightly angry. We want justice.

God is a God of justice. He is also a God of forgiveness and love. He holds these things together as Jesus died on the cross. God satisfied His justice, remaining true to His holiness, whilst demonstrating His love towards us in that while we were still sinners Christ died for us. It was at the cross of Jesus, at a place called Golgotha, where we see those three attributes of God – His holiness, His love and His justice – perfectly displayed without any contradiction or friction between them.

Power over life

But there is something more. Jesus did something you and I cannot do: He dismissed His own spirit as He prayed, 'Father, into Your hands I commit My spirit.' Earlier, Jesus had spoken remarkable words: 'No one takes [my life] from Me, but I lay it down of Myself. I have power to lay it down, and I have power to take it up again.' He had said, 'I am the life' but also that He would 'lay down' His life. Jesus is the only person who chose to die.

Of course, there are those who in tragic circumstances have taken their own life. They chose when and where and how they would die. However, eventually they, like all of us, would have died anyway. But Jesus, who is the Life-giver, who had never sinned so was not subject to death, need not have died. It was out of love for us that He gave Himself over to death, to 'taste death' for every one of us. Those who plotted to have Jesus crucified had guilty intentions and actions intending to kill Jesus, but it was Jesus Himself who dismissed His spirit and gave Himself over to death.

No other death has captured the imagination of artists, musicians, writers and preachers as the death of Jesus. It is the very heart of the Christian message. It is the main theme of the four Gospel writers – Matthew, Mark, Luke and John – who spend up to half of their writings describing the last week of the life of Jesus. They are pointing our attention to what Jesus accomplished for us when He hung on that cross. But the cross of Jesus is now empty. Jesus' story was far from ended on that first Good Friday.

5

They are the most powerful days

The greatest escape artist of all time was Harry Houdini. He was the sensation of society. It seemed that there was no way to imprison Harry. He would be put in the best jails, but in a few minutes would be out walking free. When they handcuffed him, the restraints seemed to fall off like candyfloss. They would sew him up in a canvas bag, yet he would get out. They even riveted him in huge milk churns, but again he would free himself. Out he would come from sealed and welded boilers. They put him in a coffin, wrapped chains around it, dumped it in a river and still he escaped.

Some thought he had supernatural powers saying he had the flexibility of an eel, the mind of a genius and the lives of a cat! It seemed he could escape from anything. But he died in 1926.

Houdini had wondered whether he could escape death. For a period, he had experimented with contacting the dead, with necromancy, clairvoyance and fortune telling but was convinced that they were all fakeries. And yet, he told his wife if he was to die first, he would try to contact her. He gave her a secret code. She was to sensitise her mind and be ready. For ten years on the anniversary of his death she would sit before his picture with a lit candle. Nothing ever happened. Eventually she put out the candle and never tried again.

Buried

Jesus was crucified on the day before a Sabbath. The thought of someone hanging on a cross on a sacred Jewish day was unacceptable and so the religious leaders asked Pilate to remove the bodies. Because crucified victims could hang for days on a cross gasping for breath, the soldiers speeded up the process by breaking the legs of the two thieves crucified on either side of Jesus.

That would be agony and would prevent them hoisting themselves up for breath. They would die quickly of suffocation. When the soldiers came to Jesus however, they found He had already given Himself over to death, so His legs were not broken (echoing another picture of the sacrifices in the Old Testament). But to ensure He was truly dead, professional executors thrust a spear in His side. Blood and water came out demonstrating that the pericardial sac around His heart had broken, a sure sign of death.

Friends of Jesus asked permission from Pontius Pilate to take and bury the body of Jesus. Fulfilling Old Testament prophecy, Jesus was buried in an unused tomb. His body was wrapped. There was no Turin shroud, for we are later told that Jesus' head and body were wrapped with different cloths. A huge stone was rolled in front of the grave, and then sealed. The religious leaders asked Pilate for a guard so that His body could not be stolen. A Roman guard consisted of sixteen soldiers. There Jesus' body lay.

All seemed lost. However, the best news the world has ever heard was announced in that graveyard.

Back to life

Some women who had followed Jesus were the last ones at the cross when Jesus was crucified, and they were the first ones at the tomb on the Sunday morning, planning to put burial spices on the body. There was an earthquake. Their tear-stained eyes were confronted by blazing angels.

'Do not be afraid, for I know that you seek Jesus who was crucified. He is not here; for He is risen!' an angel announced.

Soon afterwards they were to meet the risen Jesus. He too said, 'Do not be afraid'. This time there was no earthquake, and He wasn't radiating brightness. Instead, He had the scars from the crucifixion in His hands and feet and side. Awestruck, the women worshipped Him. It was the first of many appearances in various settings. On occasions He met just with one or two people, at other times with a larger group of disciples or even a crowd of over 500 people most of whom were alive some years later and could testify to what and who they saw.

Poor Thomas, one of Jesus' disciples, has been labelled as 'doubting Thomas'. On that first Easter Sunday evening, Jesus had appeared to ten of His disciples when Thomas was absent.

'Unless I see in His hands the print of the nails, and put my finger into the print of the nails, and put my hand into His side, I will not believe,' he rashly exclaimed when he was told about Jesus rising from the dead.

Days later Jesus appeared again, but this time Thomas was present. Jesus, knowing what had been said, offered His hands and side to Thomas, but Thomas fell on his knees exclaiming, 'My Lord and my God!' Jesus accepted the worship but added, 'Blessed are those who have not seen and yet have believed.'

Empty grave

One can visit the tombs of the founders of many religions, movements and political parties, but the grave of Jesus is empty. No one else has ever or will ever raise *themselves* back to life. But Jesus is risen from the dead.

Previously when Jesus' friend Lazarus had died, Jesus reassured the grieving sister, Martha, 'I am the resurrection and the life,' Jesus told her. 'He who believes in Me, though he may die, he shall live. And whoever believes in Me shall never die.' Then Jesus added the searching question, 'Do you believe this?'

'Yes, Lord,' Martha responded, 'I believe that You are the Christ, the Son of God, who is come into the world.'

The question 'Do you believe this?' is pertinent to us all.

5

They are far-reaching days

Peggy Lee was a popular American singer who is largely forgotten, but she sang a haunting melody with her smoky, husky voice whose theme has been repeated by song writers and poets for centuries. In the song, 'Is That All There Is?' she recalls how as a little girl her house caught fire and her world went up in flames, and she asked, 'Is that all there is?'

The lyrics continue: when she was twelve years old she went to the circus, but felt there was something missing, so she asked again, 'Is that all there is?' Later she fell in love with a most wonderful man. But he left her and she asked, 'Is that all there is?'

Calling death, 'that final disappointment' she thinks that when breathing her last she will still be asking, 'Is that all there is?'

Her depressing conclusion was to simply drink and dance. After all, what else can you do?

The meaning of life

The song, like so many others, misses what Jesus did that first Easter. Death is not 'the final disappointment', but rather, as the famed Yorkshire novelist, Anne Bronte, put it, death 'is but the doorway to eternal life'. Life is not meaningless. There is significance in every life lived, and in every deed done. And because Jesus has died and risen again, we can enter into a relationship with God. He is willing to forgive us and bring us to know Him in life, through death and into eternity. Jesus said that He had come to bring life and give it abundantly. The eternal life which He gives begins now and extends beyond the grave.

Jesus often spoke about life after death. He taught about heaven and hell. He made it very clear that every person is on a journey to one day meet God. In that sense every religion and life choice leads to God, but the issue is *how* we meet

Him. Will we meet God as our Father to welcome us or as our Judge to condemn us? Jesus asked a question I would wish everyone to consider:

> *For what will it profit a man if he gains the whole world and loses his own soul? Or what will a man give in exchange for his soul?*

Saved from hell

To be judged by what we have done will leave us condemned. All of us have thought, said and done wrong. None of us have kept God's commandments. Jesus said, 'For from within, out of the heart proceed evil thoughts, adulteries, fornications, murders, thefts, covetousness, wickedness, deceit …' He knows what we are like! We may be able to fool others, and maybe even ourselves, but we can never fool God. We are guilty of sins we have forgotten and of sins we wish we could forget. To be judged by God with unforgiven sin is terrible … and unnecessary.

Full of compassion and love, Jesus warned us about hell. He spoke of it as a place of outer darkness, a place of fire, a place where there would be 'weeping and gnashing of teeth'. It is horrible. Five times in just one challenging discourse He warned His hearers of the danger of being cast into hell. But God did not send His Son into the world to condemn the world but that the world might be saved. It is His love and compassion that was to take Jesus to the cross to die to purchase forgiveness for us, so that we can be ready to meet God. Jesus didn't just warn us about hell. He spoke of heaven, and promised His followers that where He is, they would one day be.

Heaven is a gift

The Bible ends with the stark contrast between heaven and hell. The youngest of Jesus' disciples, John, imprisoned for his faith on the Island of Patmos in the Mediterranean Sea, describes what God showed him:

> *Now I saw a new heaven and a new earth … God Himself will be with them and be their God. And God will wipe away every tear from their eyes; there shall be no more death, nor sorrow, nor crying. There shall be no more pain, for the former things have passed away. Then He who sat on the throne said, 'Behold, I make all things new' … But the cowardly,*

> *unbelieving, abominable, murderers, sexually immoral, sorcerers, idolaters, and all liars shall have their part in the lake which burns with fire and brimstone, which is the second death.*

There is no need for anyone to be lost in eternity. Heaven is not a reward for doing good, but a gift which Jesus purchased and offers to all. God promises heaven to everyone who turns from their own way in repentance and trusts in Jesus.

There is only one person in all history who has entered heaven on His own merit and that is Jesus. But His merit is such that anyone who trusts Him will enter because of Him. This is what the Bible calls 'grace'. It is the unmerited favour of God towards us. It was demonstrated by God at the cross and the resurrection, and it can be received as a free gift from God. Jesus did not come to call righteous people to Himself, but sinners to repentance ... and we all qualify!

God's presence

When someone 'calls on the name of the Lord' to be saved, their *past* is forgiven. God promises that He will separate our sins from us 'as far as the east is from the west'; they can be blotted out, cast 'into the depths of the sea' so that our sins and evil deeds He 'will remember no more'.

Then He promises that He will give us His Holy Spirit – in other words He will give us Himself – to be with us through all the joys and challenges of the *present*. God's help and constant presence with His people has been the experience of millions of people over 2,000 years.

The great missionary explorer, David Livingstone, had spent sixteen years in Africa but was facing great peril. At the time, he was surrounded by hostility in the heart of Africa. He was in danger of losing his life and contemplated fleeing in the night. But something happened that changed his mind and gave him peace in his perilous situation. He recorded it in his diary on 14 January 1856. He opens the account by describing his inner turmoil at the thought of a potential attack, then he writes:

> *But I read that Jesus said, 'All power is given unto me in heaven and on earth. Go, ye, therefore and teach all nations, and lo, I am with you always, even unto the end of the*

> *world.' It is the word of a gentleman and the most strict and sacred honour, so there's an end to it. I will not cross furtively tonight as I intended to. Should such a man as I flee? Nay, verily, I shall take observations for latitude and longitude tonight, though they may be the last. I feel quite calm now, thank God!*

Even in the hardest of circumstances, God will be there upholding those who trust in Him.

Three days that changed the world

As Christians spend time with God, reading the Bible, praying, getting involved with a church, and obeying and serving the Lord, they each find joy and daily purpose. God takes people as they are, but doesn't leave them that way. He begins His loving work within each Christian increasingly making each one more like Jesus. Christians are always conscious that they are not the people they want to be, nor the people they one day will be (in heaven) but they know they are not the people they once were.

And for the *future*, God will be with each person who has turned from their sin and trusted in Jesus as we go through death, and He will welcome us to His eternal home. For the Christian, the joy of heaven is to be with Jesus. He is the One who loved us and gave Himself for us on the cross. He is the One who rose from the dead, and welcomes all who will come to Him. When we turn to God Himself, we find that He has turned to us.

The three days that have changed the world have changed me, and can change you too. It begins as you ask in prayer for Jesus to become your Lord and Saviour, forgiving your past, guiding you in the present, and one day taking you to be with Himself in the future. I assure you that you will not find Him to be a disappointment.